CREATIVE DREAM INCL  TS:

LET'S DO THIS BOOK 1

A SERIES OF GUIDED JOURNALS FOR DOING YOUR IMPOSSIBLE PROJECT

YOU CAN DO THIS

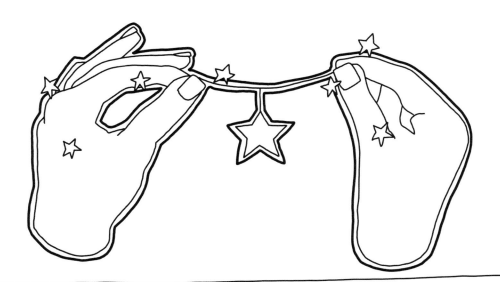

GUIDED JOURNAL FOR UNTANGLING DOUBTS, FREAKOUTS, AND AMBIVALENCE AND GETTING READY TO ACTUALLY DO YOUR PROJECT! FOR REAL!

BY ANDREA SCHROEDER

You Can Do This: Guided Journal For Untangling Doubts, Freakout, And Ambivalence And Getting Ready To actually Do Your Impossible Project! For Real! by Andrea Schroeder

@2021 Andrea Schroeder
All Rights Reserved

Book 1 from the series *Let's Do This: The Series of Guided Journals To Help You Navigate The Inner Tangles and Outer Obstacles So You Can Do Your Impossible Project.*

Creative Dream Incubator Press
www.CreativeDreamIncubator.com

Second edition, published 2021
ISBN 9798458284301

For additional material to go with this journal, sign up at:
www.CreativeDreamIncubator.com/Lets-Do-This

HI! I'M ANDREA AND I MADE THIS JOURNAL BECAUSE I BELIEVE YOUR IMPOSSIBLE PROJECT IS IMPORTANT AND I WANT TO HELP YOU MAKE IT HAPPEN.

GET FREE E-COURSES PLUS A LIVE CREATIVE GENIUS PLANNING SESSION EVERY MONDAY WHERE WE'LL WORK OUT YOUR NEXT STEPS TOGETHER!

SIGN UP HERE:
CreativeDreamIncubator.com/You-Got-This

YOUR IMPOSSIBLE PROJECT IS THAT THING YOU WANT TO DO, BUT YOU EITHER DON'T KNOW HOW TO DO IT OR YOU HAVE HUGE OBSTACLES IN YOUR WAY OR YOU'RE JUST FINDING IT HARD TO MAKE THE PROGRESS YOU WANT TO MAKE.

IMPOSSIBLE PROJECTS GROW YOU. THIS MEANS YOUR PROJECT PROBABLY IS IMPOSSIBLE - FOR THE PERSON YOU ARE TODAY. ENGAGING WITH YOUR PROJECT WILL HELP YOU BECOME MORE BRAVE, CREATIVE, AND IN TOUCH WITH YOUR INNER KNOWING. YOUR PROJECT WILL GROW YOU INTO THE VERSION OF YOU WHO CAN DO THIS.

NAMING AND CLAIMING IT
BEGINS YOUR JOURNEY ⟶
PUT YOUR PROJECT ON THE SIGN

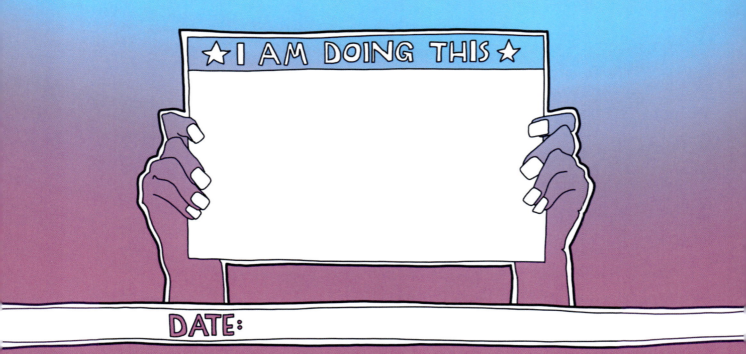

IT'S OK TO FEEL CONFLICTED
ABOUT YOUR PROJECT!

THIS IS WHY SO MANY PROJECTS
DON'T EVER GET DONE - NOT
BECAUSE THEY ARE IMPOSSIBLE, IT'S
BECAUSE THEY ARE UNCOMFORTABLE.

TO MAKE SURE THIS DOES NOT HAPPEN TO YOUR PROJECT, WE'RE GOING TO START BY MAKING SPACE TO EXPLORE ALL OF YOUR FEELINGS ABOUT YOUR PROJECT.

EVERY FEELING YOU AVOID MAKES IT HARDER TO COMPLETE YOUR PROJECT.

SO AS YOU BEGIN, REMEMBER:

IT'S FINE TO HAVE NEGATIVE THOUGHTS AND FEELINGS ABOUT YOUR PROJECT. ALL OF YOUR FEELINGS ARE A PART OF THE PROCESS.

JUST BE HONEST.

THAT'S WHERE THE ★MAGIC★ IS.

WHAT I WANT TO DO IS:

IT'S OK IF YOU DON'T KNOW EXACTLY HOW YOU WANT IT TO BE.

JUST WRITE OUT EVERYTHING YOU KNOW ABOUT IT SO FAR.

I WANT TO DO THIS BECAUSE:

WHAT I REALLY WANT TO
GET OUT OF THIS PROJECT IS:

THESE ARE THE PARTS THAT SCARE ME:

THESE ARE THE THINGS THAT HELP ME BE MORE BRAVE:

THESE ARE THE PARTS I NEED
TO LEARN MORE ABOUT:

I AM READY
TO LEARN + GROW

THESE ARE THE PARTS I FEEL SURE ABOUT:

WHAT ARE THE GIFTS, TALENTS
+ EXPERIENCE THAT YOU BRING TO
THIS PROJECT?

BE SUPER SPECIFIC!

NEXT YOU WILL EXPLORE
YOUR IDEAS ABOUT HOW TO DO
YOUR PROJECT.

GIVE EACH QUESTION SOME
THOUGHT AND FILL IN AS
MUCH AS YOU CAN.

YOUR IDEAS DO NOT HAVE
TO FEEL DO-ABLE. LET'S JUST
PLAY WITH POSSIBILITY
FOR NOW.

MY IDEAS FOR HOW
I COULD DO THIS:

IT'S FINE IF YOUR IDEAS FEEL IMPOSSIBLE RIGHT NOW.
KEEP BRAINSTORMING.

HOW WOULD YOUR BRAVEST SELF DO THIS?

WHAT IS THE EASIEST WAY YOU COULD DO THIS?

HOW DO YOU REALLY
WANT TO DO THIS?

YOUR CREATIVE GENIUS IS **BIGGER THAN** THE OBSTACLES.

THE OBSTACLES

IDEAS FOR HOW TO FACE THEM

THE OBSTACLES

IDEAS FOR HOW TO FACE THEM

WHAT KINDS OF SUPPORT SYSTEMS DOES YOUR PROJECT NEED?

WHAT KIND OF SUPPORT DO YOU NEED, TO BE ABLE TO DO YOUR PROJECT?

WHAT'S THE STORY YOU'RE TELLING YOURSELF ABOUT WHY YOU HAVEN'T DONE THIS YET?

WHAT WOULD IT TAKE
FOR YOU TO DECIDE
TO BEGIN NOW?

KEEP GOING!

IF YOU'VE FINISHED THIS JOURNAL THEN YOU ARE READY TO TAKE SOME STEPS WITH YOUR PROJECT.

GET FREE E-COURSES PLUS A LIVE CREATIVE GENIUS PLANNING SESSION EVERY MONDAY WHERE WE'LL WORK OUT YOUR NEXT STEPS TOGETHER!

SIGN UP HERE: CreativeDreamIncubator.com/You-Got-This

Made in the USA
Columbia, SC
10 August 2022

65052421R10038